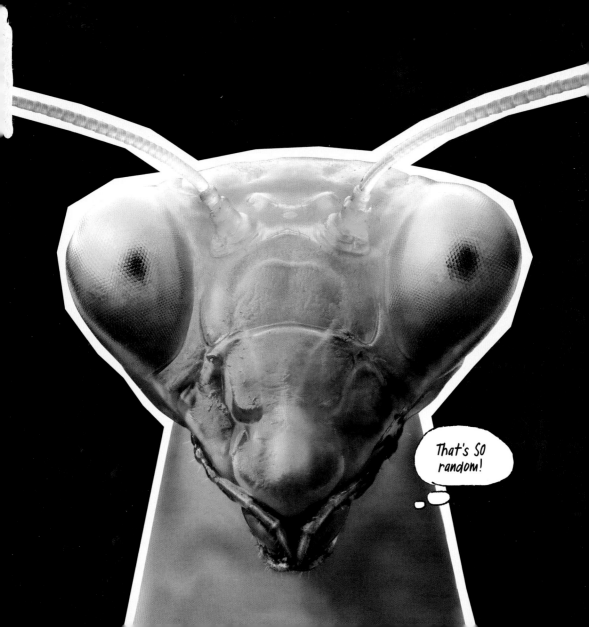

TOTALLY RANDOM QUESTIONS

QUESTIONS

VOLUME **3**

101 Strange and Stupendous Q&As

Melina Gerosa Bellows

BRIGHT MATTER BOOKS

New York

Contents

Some birds teach their babies special passwords.

∗∗4383

#1

∗∗∗783

K6p!F2lq2#

RESEARCHERS IN AUSTRALIA DISCOVERED THAT A BIRD SPECIES CALLED THE SUPERB FAIRY WREN HAS AN AMAZING WAY OF FEEDING ITS BABIES. While the babies are still growing in their eggs, **their mother teaches them a unique sound, kind of like a special "password."** She makes the sound over and over as she sits on her eggs. **After her babies hatch, they repeat the call their mother taught them.** Why does the mother do this? Well, sometimes other mother birds leave their eggs in the wren's nest for her to take care of. **By teaching her babies a special call first, a mother fairy wren can recognize her babies from those that aren't,** so she can feed her own babies first.

A baby fairy wren waiting to be fed

Over here!

Mother superb fairy wren feeding babies

About what percentage of **Earth's** land surface is covered with **ice?**

a. 1 percent

b. 10 percent

c. 25 percent

Penguins standing on an iceberg in Antarctica

NOW YOU KNOW!

At 118 miles (190 km) long, the Bering Glacier in Alaska is the longest glacier in North America.

ANSWER: b

10 percent

Instant Genius

In some areas, Antarctic ice is up to 3 miles (4.8 km) thick.

ABOUT 10 PERCENT OF EARTH IS COVERED WITH ICE, INCLUDING ICE CAPS, ICE SHEETS, AND GLACIERS. Glaciers are very slow-moving rivers of ice. Some are leftovers from the last ice age, which began about 2.6 million years ago. **Most glaciers are located in Antarctica, Greenland, and the Arctic.** A glacier that is considered small is about the size of a football field, while the **largest glacier in the world, the Lambert-Fisher Glacier in Antarctica,** is more than 250 miles (400 km) long and 60 miles (100 km) wide. Glaciers are important because they contain about 69 percent of Earth's freshwater.

12

How many bones are in the
bones are in the
human
skull?

a. 2

b. 12

c. 22

ANSWER: C 22

THE HUMAN SKULL HAS TWO MAIN FUNCTIONS: TO PROTECT THE BRAIN AND TO SUPPORT THE FACE. The cranium—the part of the skull that surrounds our brains—**is composed of eight bones. The other 14 bones, including the jaw, the nose, and the cheekbones, make up our faces. The** only bone in the skull that moves is the mandible, which you know as the jaw. **While hard skulls protect the brain, when babies are born, the skull is actually soft and in pieces. It fuses together over time**.

Instant Genius

Bones are made up of 31 percent water.

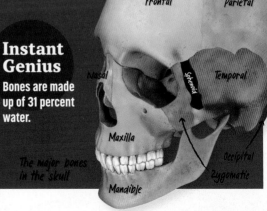

The major bones in the skull

Frontal
Parietal
Nasal
Sphenoid
Temporal
Maxilla
Occipital
Zygomatic
Mandible

14

Which Italian city **invented** modern **pizza?**

a.  Florence

b.  Naples

c. Rome

#4

Naples, Italy

ANSWER: **b**
Naples

FLATBREAD DISHES SIMILAR TO PIZZA HAVE EXISTED SINCE THE TIME OF THE ANCIENT EGYPTIANS, GREEKS, AND ROMANS. But most pizza experts agree that **Naples, Italy, is the home of the modern pizza:** a pie topped with tomato sauce and cheese and cooked in a wood-fired oven. **Antica Pizzeria Port'Alba,** which opened in Naples in 1830 and is still operating today, is said to be the **first pizza parlor in the world.**

Instant Genius
The first pizza restaurant in the United States opened in New York City in 1905.

Antica Pizzeria Port'Alba

A **praying mantis** is the only insect that can look over its shoulder.

#5

See what I mean?

ANSWER: **True**

PRAYING MANTISES ARE THE ONLY INSECTS THAT CAN TURN THEIR HEADS 180 DEGREES (HALFWAY AROUND). **A flexible joint between the head and body allows the head to swivel**—an adaptation that helps it hunt. The praying mantis earned its name for the posture it takes while waiting for prey: **As it holds its front legs in an upright position, the insect looks as if it's praying.** When something tasty comes within its reach, it quickly snatches it up and keeps a tight hold as it eats.

Instant Genius

The orchid mantis looks just like an orchid flower. Its back legs even look like petals!

What is Sacagawea known for?

#6

a. discovering America

b. inventing the dollar coin

c. interpreting Native languages for the Lewis and Clark expedition

ANSWER: C

interpreting Native languages for the Lewis and Clark expedition

Lewis and Clark with Sacagawea

FROM 1804 UNTIL 1806, EXPLORERS MERIWETHER LEWIS AND WILLIAM CLARK TRAVELED ACROSS AMERICA FROM ST. LOUIS, MISSOURI, TO WHAT IS NOW OREGON, WITH A GROUP OF MORE THAN 30 PEOPLE. Their journey very likely would not have been successful without the help of a Native American woman named Sacagawea. With her newborn baby on her back, Sacagawea explored thousands of miles with Lewis and Clark and the expedition group, starting in what is now North Dakota and traveling all the way to the Pacific coast. She acted as a peacemaker, a translator, and an interpreter between the men and other Native American peoples they met along the way. Sacagawea also rescued important journals when their expedition boat capsized, and traded horses, which allowed the expedition to cross the Rocky Mountains. Sacagawea's contributions were essential and countless.

Instant Genius

In 2000, Sacagawea's likeness was put on the dollar coin as a way of honoring her.

20

Dogs can understand both

words
and
tone
of voice.

Time for a walk!

21

SCIENTISTS HAVE LONG KNOWN THAT DOGS CAN HEAR FOUR TIMES BETTER THAN HUMANS. But new research shows **dogs might be able to understand the actual words humans use,** too! Human brains register what someone says and how they say it separately. **Scans of dogs' brains revealed that they first process the tone of a voice with one part of their brain and then process the meaning of the words with a different part—just like us!** This helps explain how a border collie named Chaser was able to learn more than 1,000 words after his owner taught him to understand language.

Instant Genius

When sniffing, dogs can breathe in and out at the same time.

#8

How did the
Golden Gate Bridge
get its name?

a. from its color

b. from the water it spans

c. to honor the California gold rush

CALIFORNIA GOLD RUSH 1849

USA

from the water it spans

THE GOLDEN GATE BRIDGE SITS OVER THE STRETCH OF WATER THAT CONNECTS THE SAN FRANCISCO BAY WITH THE PACIFIC OCEAN. This body of water is known as the **Golden Gate Strait.** It was named in 1846, just before the gold rush, by a politician and explorer who was **inspired by another landlocked harbor in Turkey called the Golden Horn of the Bosporus.** When the bridge over the strait was fully completed in 1937, it was the longest suspension bridge in the world. Originally, it was supposed to be painted blue and yellow, but when the orange primer coat was applied, the architects decided to stick with it because the **bright color made it easy for ships to spot in the fog.**

What is the largest reptile in Africa?

a. Nile monitor lizard

b. Nile crocodile

c. African rock python

#9

ANSWER: **b**

Nile crocodile

AS THE LARGEST REPTILE IN AFRICA, THE NILE CROCODILE'S
AVERAGE SIZE IS ABOUT 16 FEET (5 M) LONG AND 500
POUNDS (227 KG). Some can even grow to be 1,650 pounds
(750 kg) and up to 20 feet (6 m) long. That's quite a growth
spurt considering they **start out as small 12-inch (30-cm)-long
hatchlings!** Their main diet is fish, but these creatures will chomp
on anything in their path. **A female Nile crocodile lays eggs in
nests that she digs near riverbanks.** She guards her eggs until
they hatch, which takes about three months.

NOW
YOU KNOW!
Pollution, hunting, and
habitat loss are all threats to
the survival of Nile crocodiles.
But thanks to the work of
conservationists, their
numbers are
stable.

Why do **leaves** change color in the fall?

a. because they receive less water when the weather gets cooler

b. because of the pigment in their leaves

c. because there is too much sunlight

NOW YOU KNOW!
Not all trees change color. Evergreen trees, such as pines, stay green all year.

Burr Pond State Park, Connecticut

ANSWER: b **because of the pigment in their leaves**

LEAVES CONTAIN CHEMICALS CALLED PIGMENTS. **These pigments give leaves their colors, including greens, oranges, yellows, and reds.** During warmer seasons, when the days are longer and there is more direct sunlight, **leaves produce a green pigment called chlorophyll.** Chlorophyll masks the other pigments, turning the leaves completely green. When fall begins, the days get shorter and there is less intense sunlight. At this time of year, trees stop making chlorophyll. **As the green fades, the orange, yellow, and red shades that were there all along finally reveal themselves.**

Instant Genius
Trees help remove pollution from the air.

28

Where is the world's
longest cave system?

a. Queensland, Australia

b. Kentucky, U.S.A.

c. Moscow, Russia

Mammoth Cave National Park

ANSWER: **b**

Kentucky, U.S.A.

MAMMOTH CAVE NATIONAL PARK IN KENTUCKY, U.S.A., WAS FIRST DISCOVERED BY HUMANS MORE THAN 4,000 YEARS AGO—AND IT'S HUGE, WITH MORE THAN 400 MILES (644 KM) OF CONTINUOUS CAVES. Seven different Native American groups once used these caves as shelter during the winter or during hunting trips. Today, **many rare and endangered species live here,** including the eyeless Kentucky cave shrimp, the Indiana bat, and the gray bat. **Mammoth Cave has also been named a world wonder** and is protected as an important and unique wildlife area.

WARNING

INDIANA BAT HIBERNATING COLONY

PROHIBITED ACTIVITIES

Harassment of the Indiana Bat is prohibited by the Endangered Species Act of 1973. Harassment includes entering this cave between September 1 through March 30 or any other activities that might interfere with hibernation.

U.S. Department of the Interior
National Park Service

#12

Cats
can taste
air.

I prefer the taste of fish!

ANSWER: **True**

IF YOU SEE A CAT WITH AN OPEN MOUTH AND A STRANGE EXPRESSION ON ITS FACE—AS IF IT'S SNEERING—CHANCES ARE IT'S "TASTING" THE AIR. Goats and horses do this, too. There are tiny holes on the roof of a cat's mouth that lead to an organ in the cat's olfactory (smelling) system. A cat will open its mouth and use its tongue to "flick" the scented air toward the two holes. This allows the cat to smell and taste the air at the same time. Detecting scents help cats find prey, food, and a mate, and even mark their territory.

Instant Genius

A cat has 40 times more odor-sensing cells than humans do.

True or False:

#13

A peanut is a **nut.**

Walnut growing on a tree

EVEN THOUGH "PEANUT" HAS THE WORD *NUT* IN ITS NAME, IT'S NOT A NUT AT ALL. **It's a legume, an edible seed enclosed in a pod.** Peanuts, whose pods grow underground, are in the same family as peas, beans, lentils, and soybeans. The part of a peanut plant that grows aboveground is green and leafy and develops yellow flowers. **In general, nuts have hard outer shells you cannot eat and something inside that you can. Many nuts also grow on trees.** These include almonds, walnuts, and pecans.

NOW YOU KNOW!
Americans eat enough peanut butter each year to spread over the entire floor of the Grand Canyon!

lentils

Instant Genius
Peanuts are sometimes called "ground nuts" or "ground peas."

#14

Why does **saltwater** sting your eyes but your own tears won't?

a. Your tears don't contain any salt.

b. Your tears contain only a little salt.

c. Your tears would sting someone else's eyes, but not your own.

35

I'd rather be paid in gold!

ANSWER: b

Your tears contain only a little salt.

ALL YOUR BODY'S FLUIDS—INCLUDING BLOOD, SWEAT, TEARS, AND URINE—CONTAIN SALT. The reason your tears don't sting your eyes when they water or when you cry is because they contain **only a fraction of the salt** found in seawater. **Salt keeps the body in balance** by helping our cells absorb nutrients, keeping fluids in check, and maintaining muscle and nerve function. The body can keep or get rid of salt as needed. For example, when we're thirsty, we drink water, which dilutes the salt in our bodies. **Our kidneys get rid of any extra salt we don't need.** Although it's important not to eat too much salt, the body does need some to be able to work properly. Nutritionists suggest staying under 2,300 milligrams for teens and adults. That's about one tablespoon a day! Kids should consume even less.

How big is the world's largest type of spider?

c. about the size of a basketball

b. about the size of a softball

a. about the size of a tennis ball

ANSWER: C

about the size of a basketball

IN THE AMAZON RAINFOREST LURK SPIDERS ABOUT THE SIZE OF BASKETBALLS. The South American Goliath birdeater tarantula weighs just under half a pound (8 oz) and has an 11-inch (28-cm) leg span, making it the largest spider in the world. Despite the tarantula's name and size, it doesn't usually eat birds: Insects, frogs, rodents, and snakes are more often on the menu. And even though it has eight small eyes on the front of its head, the Goliath birdeater spider can't really see its food. Instead, it relies on the hairs covering its feet and body to detect prey. Once it finds something to eat, it sinks its 1-inch (2.5-cm)-long venom-filled fangs into the creature and drags it back to its burrow under the forest floor.

NOW YOU KNOW!
Many spiders liquefy their prey by releasing an enzyme into the insides of their soon-to-be meal. Then, the spider sucks out the juice. The outside of the prey is usually left alone.

The largest diamond

in the world is in outer space.

ANSWER: True

DIAMONDS ARE THE HARDEST NATURAL SUBSTANCE ON EARTH. But the largest known diamond isn't in a jewelry store or museum on Earth—it's in outer space, about 50 million light-years away. **This space diamond is estimated to be 2,500 miles (4,000 km) across and about 10 billion-trillion-trillion-carats in size—that's a 10 followed by 33 zeros!** Technically known as **BPM 37093, it has been renamed "Lucy" by astronomers** after the Beatles song, "Lucy in the Sky with Diamonds."

Where's the snow?

True or False:

Penguins live in Africa.

#17

41

Boulders Beach, Cape Town, South Africa

Instant Genius
Penguins have waterproof feathers.

I've only seen snow in the movies!

NOW YOU KNOW!
African penguins have a pattern of dots across their chests. These patterns are unique to each individual penguin.

ANSWER: **True**

African penguin

PENGUINS ARE FOUND ACROSS THE SOUTHERN HEMISPHERE, LIVING EVERYWHERE FROM AFRICA TO SOUTH AMERICA TO AUSTRALIA. And, of course, a number of penguin species, including Adélie and emperor penguins, live in Antarctica. A species known as the **African penguin lives along the rocky southeastern and southwestern coasts of Africa,** from the countries of Mozambique to Namibia, and also on nearby islands. The environment there is warm, and the sun's heat can be very harsh, so one of the ways **African penguins stay cool is by building their nests under the shade of rocks and bushes.**

How long is the average pit stop during a Formula One race?

a. 3.27 seconds

b. 32.7 seconds

c. 3 minutes and 27 seconds

Louis Zborowski passing Humphrey Cook by skidding above him, Brooklands racetrack.

ANSWER: a   3.27 seconds

Designing a Formula One engine

FORMULA ONE IS A SERIES OF INTERNATIONAL AUTO RACES. ("Formula" refers to the specific set of rules each car must follow to participate.) **Each individual race, called a Grand Prix, features the fastest cars in the world.** Each Grand Prix is held in a different country, including Monaco, Japan, and Italy. **The races are usually at least 190 miles (300 km) of continuous driving at high speeds around a circuit,** which takes about two hours. When the cars need a pit stop, the team works as fast as possible to make fixes, such as changing tires, to get the car back on the road and into the race. **On average, these pit stops take less than 4 seconds!**

Instant Genius

Each Formula One car has an average of 80,000 parts.

Only female
mosquitoes bite.

#19

Tasty...good!

ANSWER: **True**

BEFORE FEMALE MOSQUITOES PRODUCE EGGS, THEY BECOME TINY VAMPIRES: They need the nutrition blood contains to make their eggs. **To help them locate a host, female mosquitoes have a special organ that detects the carbon dioxide we exhale, the temperature of our bodies, and even scents, such as body odor.** Your skin gets itchy after a mosquito bite because the substance in the female's bite that stops your blood from clotting causes an allergic reaction.

NOW YOU KNOW!

Mosquitoes have been on Earth for about 210 million years—since the Jurassic period, when dinosaurs such as *Brachiosaurus* and *Allosaurus* roamed the planet.

Which is one of the top three **most dangerous** jobs in America?

#20

a. commercial fishing

b. firefighting

c. ambulance driving

Crab fisherman in the Bering Sea, Alaska

ANSWER: a

commercial fishing

logging tools

MANY PEOPLE FIND FISHING A RELAXING WAY TO SPEND TIME. **But for commercial fishers who go out to sea, fishing is one of the most dangerous jobs around.** Why? Ferocious storms on the seas, icy waters, and being out in the open ocean far from doctors and hospitals are all factors that make it a risky profession. **Another job in the top three most dangerous is logging.** Loggers cut trees to provide wood so that the wood can be made into different materials such as paper or furniture. They use heavy, dangerous machines to do their work. Derrick operators who mine and drill for oil and gas also have one of the most dangerous jobs in the United States. Like loggers, they use large and very heavy equipment (derricks and drills) to do their work extracting materials from the ground. If used incorrectly, this equipment can be very hazardous and even fatal. **The least risky jobs include working as an educator or a librarian.**

How old was the
oldest
person
who ever
lived?

a. 102 years old

b. 112 years old

c. 122 years old

NOW YOU KNOW!

The oldest living land animal is a giant tortoise named Jonathan. He is estimated to be 189 years old.

ANSWER: c 122 years old

Jeanne Calment

WHILE IT'S POSSIBLE THAT SOMEONE HAS LIVED LONGER, THE OLDEST PERSON ON RECORD WAS A FRENCH WOMAN NAMED JEANNE CALMENT, WHO LIVED TO BE 122. Jeanne was born in 1875 and passed away in 1997. During her life, she was known for playing the piano and participating in athletics like fencing, roller skating, tennis, swimming, and cycling. **She also ate a diet rich in olive oil and chocolate, which can be good for health in moderate amounts.** In her lifetime, Calment witnessed the invention of the car, the computer, and the Internet. **Guinness World Records had already recognized her as the world's oldest person when she was "only" 112.** She managed to beat her own record, one that still stands today.

Instant Genius

The average person's life expectancy in the United States is 78.8 years old.

#22

True or False:

Sharks
must swim continuously to keep breathing.

51

Gray Reef Shark, Solomon Islands

ANSWER: **False**

SHARKS ARE FOUND IN EVERY OCEAN HABITAT, INCLUDING THE DEEP SEA, CORAL REEFS, AND UNDER ARCTIC ICE.
Some of the more than 500 species of sharks must keep swimming to stay alive. **They take in oxygen by allowing water to pass over their gills and through their open mouths as they swim.** If they stop moving, so does the flow of oxygen-rich water. **Great whites, whale sharks, and makos get oxygen this way. But not all shark species need to keep swimming so they can keep breathing.** The majority of sharks use cheek muscles to pump water into their mouths and over their gills to keep oxygen flowing. These sharks, which include nurse and bullheads, can take a break from swimming to rest on the ocean floor because their respiratory system will do the work.

Instant Genius

The dwarf lantern shark is the smallest shark in the world. It's smaller than an adult human hand!

Why do people drive on the left side of the road in Great Britain?

GREAT BRITAIN

DRIVING LICENCE

a. because it's safer

b. to keep traffic moving

c. to keep the right hand free

#23

53

NOW YOU KNOW!

People in India, South Africa, Australia, and other former British territories also drive on the left side of the road.

Oxford Road, Manchester City, UK

ANSWER: C

to keep the right hand free

Instant Genius

The Toyota Corolla is the most popular car in the world.

TRAVELING ON THE LEFT SIDE OF THE ROAD DATES BACK THOUSANDS OF YEARS, TO THE TIMES OF ANCIENT GREEKS, EGYPTIANS, AND ROMANS. Back then—long before cars were invented—everyone had to be prepared to defend themselves as they traveled along different routes. **Nearly 90 percent of people were right-handed, so keeping the right hand free to take on an opponent passing on your left was thought to be safer and more effective.** Many centuries later, in 1835, the British government made it a law to drive on the left. **Most of the world's drivers today use the right-hand side of the road.**

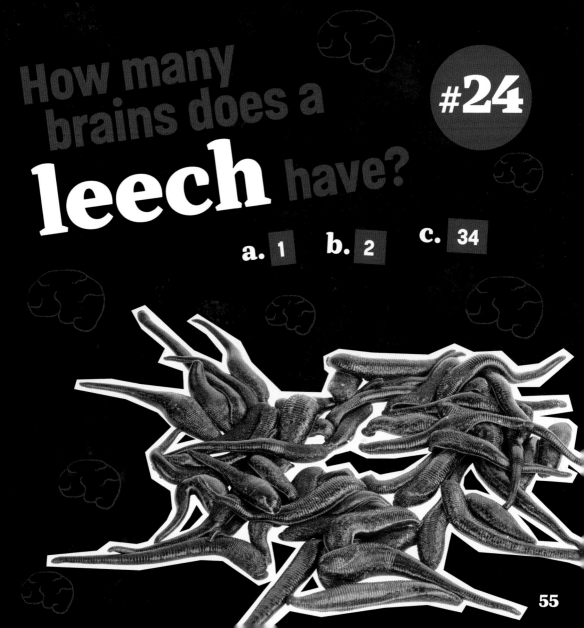

How many brains does a **leech** have?

#24

a. 1 b. 2 c. 34

55

Instant Genius

Leeches have a proboscis, a long tubelike structure that they use to suck blood from their hosts.

ANSWER: **C** **34**

Anyone know why my nose itches?

A LEECH IS AN ANNELID, WHICH IS A TYPE OF WORM. Leech bodies have 34 segments—and each segment has its own type of brain. As carnivores, many eat meat. Some eat hamsters, frogs, and bats. **Many species of leeches also suck the blood of mammals, including humans.** One such species lives inside the noses of camels in the desert. **As gross as it seems, doctors have been using leeches to treat patients since medieval times.**

Where were the first apple trees grown in North America?

a. the Northwest

b. the Northeast

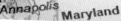

c. the South

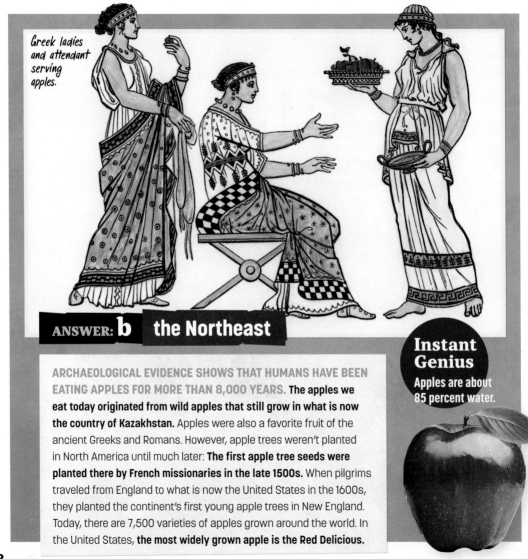

Greek ladies and attendant serving apples.

ANSWER: b the Northeast

ARCHAEOLOGICAL EVIDENCE SHOWS THAT HUMANS HAVE BEEN EATING APPLES FOR MORE THAN 8,000 YEARS. **The apples we eat today originated from wild apples that still grow in what is now the country of Kazakhstan.** Apples were also a favorite fruit of the ancient Greeks and Romans. However, apple trees weren't planted in North America until much later: **The first apple tree seeds were planted there by French missionaries in the late 1500s.** When pilgrims traveled from England to what is now the United States in the 1600s, they planted the continent's first young apple trees in New England. Today, there are 7,500 varieties of apples grown around the world. In the United States, **the most widely grown apple is the Red Delicious.**

Instant Genius

Apples are about 85 percent water.

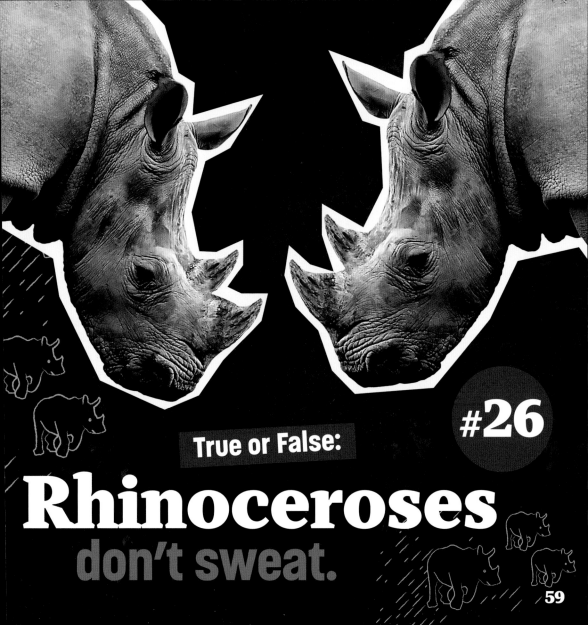

True or False:

Rhinoceroses
don't sweat.

#26

African white rhino

ANSWER: True

Instant Genius
Rhino horns are made from keratin, the same stuff as your fingernails.

RHINOS ARE NATIVE TO AFRICA AND SOUTHERN ASIA. Though they live in a hot climate, these thick-skinned animals don't sweat. To stay cool, they rest in the shade or chill out in muddy ponds. The mud serves as sunblock, and soaking protects their skin from insects. **Rhinos have poor eyesight, so they rely on their sense of smell to get around.** They are also herbivores, which means they eat only plants. Because they are so large, they must eat up to 120 pounds (54 kg) of vegetation a day, but they can survive up to five days without water.

#27

Ireland
has no
**native
snakes.**

61

Dunluce Castle, Northern Ireland

ANSWER: True

THE REASON THERE ARE NO NATIVE SNAKES IN IRELAND IS BECAUSE OF THE COUNTRY'S PAST CLIMATE. **The most recent ice age, which was about 10,000 years ago, made the environment too cold for snakes to survive there.** When all the ice melted, the land that is now the Republic of Ireland and Northern Ireland became an island surrounded by water—**permanently keeping the snakes away.** Ireland's neighbor Great Britain—which is also an island—does have snakes. This is because England was once connected to the mainland of Europe thousands of years ago by a piece of land. The land bridge eventually flooded, but the snakes that had made it across before that were able to survive.

Instant Genius

New Zealand, Iceland, Greenland, and Antarctica also have no native snake species.

Antarctica

#28

How many
faces does a
**soccer
ball**
have?

a. 26

b. 32

c. 48

ANSWER: b   32

A SOCCER BALL IS A TRUNCATED ICOSAHEDRON. What is that exactly? Well, it's **a shape with 32 faces,** and that's what a soccer ball has. **Making up 20 of these faces are hexagons, which have 6 sides. The other 12 faces are pentagons, which have 5 sides.** The different interlocking shapes form the ball, allowing it to roll around evenly when it hits the ground and maintain its speed for a longer period of time.

Instant Genius

One of the first women's soccer clubs was started in 1895 in England.

True or False:

The planet

Uranus

rotates upside down.

#29

Uranus

URANUS DOESN'T ROTATE UPSIDE DOWN, BUT IT DOES ROTATE ON ITS SIDE. IT IS THE ONLY PLANET IN OUR SOLAR SYSTEM THAT ROTATES THIS WAY. Scientists think an object twice the size of Earth crashed into Uranus a long time ago, causing it to effectively "topple over." It takes 84 Earth years for Uranus to make just one orbit around the sun, so each of the planet's four seasons lasts 21 years. In summer and winter, one of the planet's poles is always facing the sun. **The side facing the sun is always light, and the side facing away from the sun is always dark.**

Venus

Instant Genius

Our solar system is home to at least five dwarf planets: Ceres, Pluto, Makemake, Haumea, and Eris.

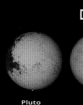

Dwarf planets

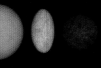

Pluto   Eris   Haumea Makemake Ceres

NOW YOU KNOW!

Both Uranus and Venus rotate from east to west— backward compared with all the other planets in our solar system, which spin from west to east.

Where is the smallest country in the world located?

#30

a. in the Caribbean Sea

b. in Italy

c. in Asia

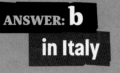

THE SMALLEST COUNTRY IN THE WORLD IS VATICAN CITY, WHICH IS LOCATED WITHIN THE CITY OF ROME, ITALY. Vatican City is home to the headquarters of the Roman Catholic Church and to the country's head of state, known as the pope. **With a population of about 1,000 people, Vatican City has an area of less than 1 square mile (2.5 sq km).** People there speak a variety of languages, including Italian, Latin, and French. **This tiny country mints its own money, makes its own stamps, and even issues its own license plates and passports.**

Instant Genius

You could fit almost eight Vatican Cities within New York City's Central Park.

69

ANSWER: True

IF YOU'VE EVER FELT GUILTY ABOUT NOT SHARING YOUR FAVORITE DESSERT WITH YOUR CAT, YOU DON'T NEED TO: According to new research, cats lack the taste buds for sweetness. Turns out one of the two receptors needed to detect the taste of sweet was switched off millions of years ago because sugar wasn't an important or essential part of cats' diets. Ever since then, big cats (like lions and tigers) and house cats have been primarily meat-eaters, known as carnivores. According to scientists, cats are the only mammals lacking the sweet gene. Close relatives of the cat, such as the mongoose and the hyena, can detect sweet tastes.

Tabby kitten

#32

Michael Phelps

has won more Olympic gold medals than any other athlete.

71

Rio de Janeiro 2016 Olympic Games

PHELPS

ANSWER: **True**

MICHAEL PHELPS HAS WON A TOTAL OF 23 GOLD MEDALS, ALL FOR SWIMMING. This is more than twice the amount of any other Olympic athlete! Phelps started his gold medal winning streak in Athens, Greece, in 2004. At the **Beijing Olympics in 2008, he won eight more.** Phelps added more gold medals to his collection when he **won four gold during the London Olympics in 2012 and five at the Rio Olympics in 2016.** Phelps started swimming for the U.S. Olympic Team in 2000. He was only 15 years old and the youngest American male swimmer in almost 70 years to compete at the Olympics.

Dalmatian

puppies are born with spots.

#33

73

WHEN DALMATIAN PUPPIES ARE BORN, THEY'RE ALL WHITE. But the skin under the fur already has the dark pigment in areas where their spots will show. After two weeks, the fur growing over the pigmented skin will start to grow in dark. **These spots continue to develop for a few more months, at which point they're fully visible.** Usually, the spots—a pattern known as piebald—are black or brown, but they can also be yellow or a bluish gray color. **No two Dalmatians have the same set of spots.**

Instant Genius

Dalmatians have spots on the inside of their mouths, too.

NOW YOU KNOW!

Wall paintings of spotted dogs have been found in ancient Egyptian tombs.

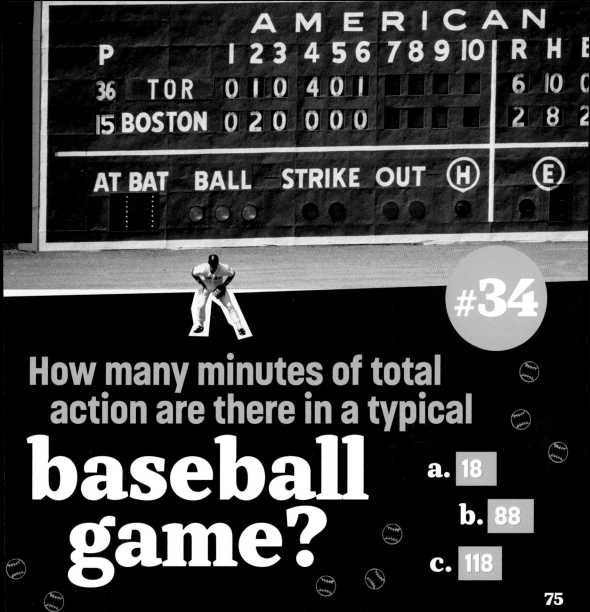

How many minutes of total action are there in a typical baseball game?

#34

a. 18

b. 88

c. 118

75

ANSWER: a 18

A TYPICAL BASEBALL GAME HAS NINE INNINGS. Each inning usually lasts 20 minutes, so the whole game lasts for about three hours. Fans love to watch all the balls-in-play action, including strikeouts, wild pitches, stolen bases, and of course, home runs. **But it turns out that 90 percent of the time, players—not to mention fans—are waiting for the action.** What's with all the waiting? It turns out that a lot of time goes by between pitches. The batter stepping into the box, the catcher going out to the mound to talk to the pitcher, and the pause between pitches all add up to a lot of downtime. **But it's probably a good thing for the sales hot dogs, popcorn, and lemonade!**

Sphenopalatine ganglioneuralgia

can kill you.

#35

ANSWER: **False**

CHANCES ARE YOU'VE FACED DOWN SPHENOPALATINE GANGLIONEURALGIA AND SURVIVED PERFECTLY FINE. More commonly known as "brain freeze" or an ice cream headache, this common condition is most often **caused by sweet treats such as ice cream or Popsicles!** It's your brain's way of telling you to slow down the consumption of your cold treat. When something cold hits the roof of your mouth or the back of your throat, it can trigger a nerve that carries sensory information to your brain. **The sudden cold causes blood vessels to tighten.** Your body then sends more blood to warm up the affected area. This rush of blood causes blood vessels to swell. **The instant headache, which usually lasts for 20 to 30 seconds, is caused by the combination of the blood vessel tightening and then the new rush of blood.**

Instant Genius

It takes 3 gallons (11.4 L) of milk to make 1 gallon (3.8 L) of ice cream.

Which country has the most pyramids?

a. **Egypt**

b. **Peru**

c. **Sudan**

ANSWER: **C** **Sudan**

Ancient Meroë pyramids, Sudan

IT'S ALMOST IMPOSSIBLE TO THINK OF EGYPT WITHOUT PICTURING ITS FAMOUS PYRAMIDS. Many other ancient cultures—including the ancient Greeks, the Aztecs, and the Maya—built pyramids, too. These were used mainly as tombs for kings and queens. What might be surprising, though, is that the African country of Sudan is home to even more pyramids than Egypt. **There are more than 220 in Sudan, compared with about 120 in Egypt.** Known as the Nubian pyramids, these structures were built 1,000 years after the Egyptian pyramids.

Pyramid, Sphinx, Egypt

Newborn giraffes have horns.

#37

81

Instant Genius

At about 6 feet (1.8 m) in height, newborn giraffes are taller than most humans.

NOW YOU KNOW!

Male okapis also have ossicones. Okapis are related to giraffes, but live in the African rainforests instead of the savanna.

ANSWER: False

GIRAFFES HAVE HORNLIKE PROTRUSIONS ON THEIR HEADS CALLED OSSICONES, which are formed from cartilage and covered in skin. But when a baby giraffe is born, the ossicones are not yet grown in. **This helps keep the mother and baby safe while the baby is being delivered.** The ossicones develop later, as the baby matures. Male and females both have ossicones, but a female's ossicones are thinner.

Which is the tallest waterfall?

a. Niagara Falls

c. Victoria Falls (Mosi-oa-Tunya)

b. Angel Falls (Kerepakupai Merú)

Angel Falls, Venezuela

ANSWER: b

Angel Falls (Kerepakupai Merú)

ANGEL FALLS, THE WORLD'S TALLEST WATERFALL ON LAND, IS LOCATED IN THE SOUTH AMERICAN COUNTRY OF VENEZUELA. With a height of 3,212 feet (979 m), it's 17 times the height of Horseshoe Falls, the largest of the three waterfalls that make up Niagara Falls. That's pretty tall, but Earth's tallest waterfall of all is actually in the ocean. Located between Greenland and Iceland, the waterfall—known as the Denmark Strait cataract —is 11,500 feet (3,505 m) tall—and it's all underwater!

Horseshoe Falls, Canada

NOW YOU KNOW!
The Indigenous name for Angel Falls is Kerepakupai Merú.

Instant Genius
Niagara Falls spans across the border of New York, U.S.A., and Ontario, Canada.

84

When was the toilet paper roll invented?

#39

a. 850

b. 1890

c. 1940

ANSWER: **b** 1890

IN ANCIENT TIMES, WHEN PEOPLE WENT TO THE
BATHROOM, THEY USED WATER AND SNOW TO CLEAN
THEMSELVES, BUT ALSO USED SHELLS, STONES,
STICKS, SEA SPONGES, ANIMAL FURS, AND EVEN
CORNCOBS. In the mid-1800s, rough little squares
called "medicated paper" were made and sold in a box of
500 sheets. Then, in 1890, the Scott Paper Company of
Philadelphia, Pennsylvania, invented the toilet paper roll
pierced with holes around a cardboard tube. At the time,
a roll of 1,000 sheets sold for only 10 cents. The Scotts
brand of toilet paper is still sold today, along with many
other brands.

Instant
Genius
The cardboard tube in the
center of the toilet paper
is called the core.

86

40

True or False:

Butterflies
live on every continent.

ANSWER: False

THERE ARE ABOUT 17,500 SPECIES OF BUTTERFLIES FOUND ON EVERY CONTINENT EXCEPT ANTARCTICA. Like all insects, butterflies are cold-blooded, meaning they can't regulate their own body temperature. They must rely on the temperature of their environment to stay warm enough to fly, so they typically live in tropical climates. In general, butterflies can't fly if it is colder than 55°F (13°C). Monarch butterflies are the only species of butterfly that migrate round-trip. The monarchs that live in the eastern part of the United States and Canada go south to Mexico for the winter. Monarchs that live in the western United States and Canada go to Southern California.

#41

The fastest human

in the world has legs of two different lengths.

ANSWER: True

USAIN BOLT, WHOSE NICKNAME IS "LIGHTNING BOLT," HOLDS THE RECORD FOR BEING THE FASTEST SPRINTER IN THE WORLD. He earned 8 Olympic gold medals and 11 world championship titles. Bolt, who is from Jamaica, is the world record holder for the 100-meter, 200-meter, and 4x100-meter relays. He also has scoliosis, a condition that causes the spine to curve, which can affect the entire body. For Bolt, the condition causes his right leg to be shorter than his left leg. Despite his scoliosis, Bolt broke incredible records and never let it hold him back!

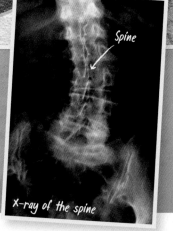

Spine

X-ray of the spine

#42

True or False:

Birds

are the only animals
that migrate.

Humpback whales make the longest migration of any mammal.

Cannonball!

ANSWER: **False**

CERTAIN SPECIES OF EVERY MAJOR ANIMAL GROUP MIGRATE, INCLUDING BIRDS, MAMMALS, FISH, REPTILES, AMPHIBIANS, AND INVERTEBRATES. Animals travel long distances to find food and warmer climates in the winter, or to mate. **Herds of wildebeests can stretch 25 miles (40 km) across the African Serengeti** as they make their migration journey each year to find fresh grass to eat. **Salmon use their sense of smell and Earth's magnetic field to navigate** their way back to the streams and rivers where they were born. **And humpback whales travel more than 9,000 miles (14,500 km) round-trip:** During the summer, they feed in cold waters of the northern parts of the oceans. In the winter, they move south to warmer waters where female humpbacks give birth to their calves.

NOW YOU KNOW!

The artic tern holds the record for longest distance migration. It travels about 18,600 miles (30,000 km) round-trip from the Arctic to the Antarctic. Over its lifetime, this bird migrates a distance that equals three round-trips to the moon!

How many stars are in the
Big Dipper?

#43

a. 7   **b.** 10   **c.** 14

ANSWER: **a** 7

CONSTELLATIONS ARE GROUPS OF STARS THAT MAKE IMAGINARY PICTURES IN THE NIGHT SKY. **Part of a larger constellation known as the Great Bear, the Big Dipper is an asterism, which is a prominent group of stars.** The Big Dipper is one of the most familiar star shapes in the northern sky, usually easy to find because the stars are close to one another and have about the same level of brightness. **It is believed that the name "Big Dipper" came from Africa, where people thought that the seven stars looked like a drinking gourd—a ladle-like tool used for scooping liquids.**

NOW YOU KNOW!
The Big Dipper goes by different names depending on the culture. In the United Kingdom and Ireland, it's called the Plough. In Malaysia it's called Buruj Biduk, or the Ladle.

True or False:

The oldest known **valentine** dates back to the 1800s.

#44

95

St. Valentine

Geoffrey Chaucer

ANSWER: False

A MEDIEVAL POET NAMED GEOFFREY CHAUCER IS THOUGHT TO HAVE BEEN THE FIRST TO RECORD MID-FEBRUARY AS A TIME TO CELEBRATE ROMANCE. He mentioned "Seynt Valentyne's Day" in one of his poems in the late 14th century. **The oldest known paper valentine dates back to the 1400s.** Housed at London's British Library and written in French, the love note was a poem written by a young duke who was imprisoned in the Tower of London to his wife. **Later, in 18th-century England, couples began to give one another candy, flowers, and love notes to show their affection**.

Instant Genius

People spend millions of dollars on their pets each Valentine's Day.

love you more!

Why do **crackers** have holes in them?

a. to keep them flat while they bake

b. to help cheese and spreads stick better to them

c. so that they don't look like cookies

ANSWER: a

to keep them flat while they bake

THE LITTLE PINPRICKS IN CRACKERS ARE CALLED DOCKING HOLES. **These holes allow air to escape while crackers are baking.** Without the holes, air would stay in the dough and the crackers would expand and become puffy, like a biscuit. **Crackers were invented in 1792 and became popular with sailors because they didn't spoil on ships as quickly as bread did.** But they weren't named crackers until 1801, when a batch was accidentally overcooked and the burning made a crackling noise. Since then, the name has stuck.

African bullfrogs

have been observed attacking lions.

 #46

Bullies beware!

Nap time!

ANSWER: True

AFRICAN BULLFROGS ARE ONE OF THE LARGEST FROGS IN THE WORLD AND THE LARGEST FROG FOUND IN SOUTHERN AFRICA. Some males reach 9 inches (23 cm)—about the size of a small pizza. African bullfrogs are carnivores, consuming birds, reptiles, small rodents, and even other frogs and amphibians. **They are also aggressive: When provoked, they have been known to attack lions and even elephants!** The frog can inflate its body and attack with its huge open mouth. Its bite is so strong that it can dent a broomstick.

Instant Genius
Female African bullfrogs lay 3,000 to 4,000 eggs at a time.

What was **bubble wrap** first used for?

a. protective headgear

c. wallpaper

b. pet clothing

ANSWER: C

wallpaper

BUBBLE WRAP WAS INVENTED ACCIDENTALLY BY TWO SCIENTISTS IN 1957, AFTER THEY SEALED TWO PLASTIC SHOWER CURTAINS TOGETHER AND SOME AIR BUBBLES GOT TRAPPED. The engineers tried to sell their unusual creation as decorative, three-dimensional wallpaper. That plan failed, but soon after, IBM needed a way to safely ship and protect their new computers. **They started shipping computers wrapped in bubble wrap to customers who had never encountered the strange material.** Before long, people started to burst the little bubbles, enjoying the satisfying *pop* sound they make. **Today, bubble wrap is used to pack everything from dishes to electronics.**

FROM PLASTICS HEADQUARTERS —

LAMINATED MATERIALS *for Countless Services*

BAKELITE

PLASTICS HEADQUARTERS

Instant Genius

Plastic was invented in 1907.

Why do your fingers wrinkle when you spend a lot of time in the water?

a. They are waterlogged.

b. Blood vessels have constricted.

c. Water dehydrates the skin.

103

NOW
YOU KNOW!
Macaques, a type of
primate, are the only other
animal that scientists know
to experience wrinkly
fingers when they
get wet.

I should be a hand model!

ANSWER: **b**

Blood vessels have constricted.

WHEN FINGERS AND TOES SHRIVEL UP TO LOOK LIKE OLD PRUNES AFTER A LONG BATH OR SWIM, IT'S JUST A SIGN THAT YOUR BODY IS FUNCTIONING PROPERLY. The fancy name for this is vasoconstriction, meaning that the blood vessels just below the surface of the skin have shrunk, leaving the skin a little baggy. This can happen after just five minutes in the water! It occurs only on certain parts of the body, including fingers, palms, toes, and the soles of the feet. **Scientists have discovered that human skin shrinking may actually be a helpful adaptation.** Turns out, it's easier to grip wet things when our fingers are prunelike: **The same way a car's tire treads help it grip the road, the little ridges in our skin help keep wet objects from slipping from our hands.**

Instant Genius

Baby elephants are born wrinkly so that they have extra skin to grow into as they age.

There are more countries named after women than men.

Paradise Beach, Saint Lucia

ANSWER: **False**

THERE ARE 195 INDEPENDENT COUNTRIES IN THE WORLD. And some of them are named after people—but only one is named after a woman. The Caribbean island nation of **Saint Lucia, also known as Saint Lucie, was named after Saint Lucy of Syracuse by a group of French seamen** who were shipwrecked on the island in 1502. **It's home to an active volcano and lush rainforests that are filled with wildlife, including bats, wild pigs, 12 species of lizards, and 157 species of birds.** The coral reefs surrounding Saint Lucia attract dolphins, whales, and several species of sea turtles.

Saint Lucy

NOW YOU KNOW!

Saint Lucy of Syracuse is considered the patron saint of sight by some Christians.

What is the
longest animal
in the world?

a. **a whale**

b. **a worm**

c. **a snake**

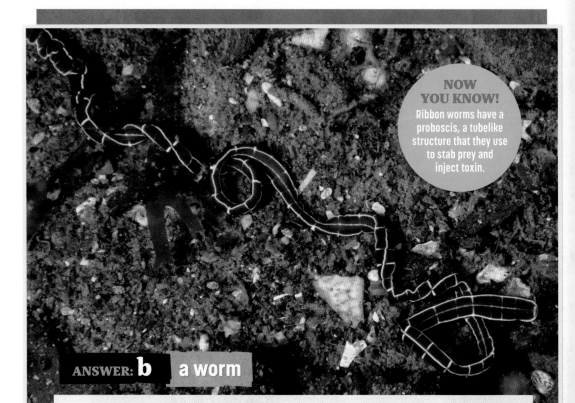

ANSWER: b **a worm**

THERE ARE MORE THAN 1,300 SPECIES OF RIBBON WORMS THAT LIVE ALL OVER THE WORLD, AND THEY COME IN ALL SHAPES AND SIZES. **The largest species, the bootlace worm, can grow to be more than 150 feet (46 m) long, which is about the same length as four school buses lined up end to end!** Though they can be very long, ribbon worms are only 1 inch (2.5 cm) wide. Ribbon worms mostly live in the ocean but can also live in freshwater or even on land. They look like long, skinny pieces of spaghetti, sometimes brightly colored or striped. Ribbon worms move by gliding over the bottom of the ocean using slime and tiny hairs called cilia. **Despite their soft, squishy appearance, ribbon worms are voracious eaters who prey on clams, crabs, fish, and worms.**

How many different items are for sale in an average

American grocery store?

a. **2,800**

b. **28,000**

c. **280,000**

THE TYPICAL GROCERY STORE STOCKS AN AVERAGE OF 28,000 DIFFERENT PRODUCTS. **The three top-selling items are soda, milk, and bread. On a typical day, 32 million Americans will head to a grocery store.** The average person in America makes a trip to the store 1.6 times a week and spends about 41 minutes shopping. That adds up to about 57 hours a year! **The most popular day of the week to go grocery shopping is Saturday,** and most shoppers go before lunch.

NOW YOU KNOW!

People who shop during the week instead of on the weekend spend an average of seven minutes less in the grocery store.

Instant Genius

Frozen foods first hit grocery stores in 1930.

ANSWER: True

THE AUTOBAHN IS GERMANY'S SUPERHIGHWAY. **With a total length of 7,500 miles (12,000 km), it is one of the longest roadways in the world ... and about 70 percent of it has no speed limit!** The autobahn was specifically designed for high-speed travel, with wider lanes and curves and no crossing traffic. There are some rules, however. **Drivers must slow down when passing through construction zones and populated areas or when there's bad weather.** Other than that, drivers can move as fast as their cars can take them.

Instant Genius

Construction to build the first section of the autobahn began in 1929.

Autobahn, Germany

How many hours a day do house cats sleep?

#53

a. 6 to 10 hours

b. 13 to 17 hours

c. 15 to 20 hours

Zzzzzzzzzzzz!

Ah, nice and cozy.

ANSWER: b

13 to 17 hours

HOUSE CATS TYPICALLY SLEEP ABOUT 13 TO 17 HOURS A DAY. **In the wild, cats sleep long hours to recharge for their next hunt.** Domesticated cats do the same because, genetically, they're programmed the same way. **Cats have a few classic snoozing positions.** The most popular way is curled up in a ball. This helps them conserve heat and protect themselves. **Cats also love to sleep in boxes and small spaces because it makes them feel secure.** If you notice whiskers or paws twitching, your cat is probably having a dream.

What is **Florence Nightingale** known for?

a. **being a bird-watcher**

b. **being a nurse**

c. **being the first female mathematician**

Florence Nightingale started a school for nursing in 1860.

ANSWER: b **being a nurse**

FLORENCE NIGHTINGALE WAS BORN INTO A WEALTHY BRITISH FAMILY IN 1820. She wasn't expected to work when she grew up, but from an early age, she wanted to become a nurse. So in 1844, Florence went to nursing school in Germany. After she finished, she went back to London, England, and got to work. **She was soon asked to help at a military hospital in eastern Europe. When she first arrived, the hospital was filthy. Florence knew that the soldiers were dying from their battle wounds, but she also believed that diseases such as typhoid and cholera, which spread due to a lack of cleanliness, were making things worse.** Florence and her team cleaned the hospital, which helped stop the spread of those diseases. Afterward, **Florence wrote a report about her experience and the effect of improving the cleanliness of military hospitals.** This report helped change the way British military hospitals were run. Today, she is known as the mother of modern nursing.

#55

How do polar bears stay warm in winter?

a. They have hollow hairs that insulate their bodies.

b. They migrate a little farther south.

c. They roll around for hours at a time.

ANSWER: a

They have hollow hairs that insulate their bodies.

Instant Genius

Polar bears use their large front paws to paddle with when they swim.

POLAR BEARS ARE UNIQUELY ADAPTED TO THEIR HARSH ARCTIC ENVIRONMENT. A bear's light-colored coat blends into its snowy habitat. Though this coat appears white to our eyes, their hair is **actually clear and hollow**. This hollow hair helps insulate the bears from the cold by allowing sunlight to reach their black skin underneath. Their dark skin can then absorb the sun's heat. **They also have a thick layer of fat and a coat that is double-layered to help keep them warm both on land and when swimming in frigid waters.** A polar bear's body is so good at keeping it warm that it needs to be careful not to overheat!

How many moons does Jupiter have?

#56

a. 39   b. 59   c. 79

Instant Genius
Ganymede is larger than the planet Mercury.

ANSWER: **c** **79**

SOME PLANETS HAVE SEVERAL MOONS. SOME, LIKE MERCURY AND VENUS, DON'T HAVE ANY. Jupiter has 79, and this number might change to 80, as a new moon was recently discovered but has not been made official yet. Jupiter also has the biggest moon in our solar system. **Its name is Ganymede, and you can spot it in the night sky with a pair of binoculars. Scientists think Ganymede is made up of three layers: an iron core, a mantle made of rock, and a layer of ice on its surface.** Saturn is the only planet with more moons than Jupiter. It has 82! Saturn's moon Titan is the second largest in our solar system.

Galileo

NOW YOU KNOW!
Galileo discovered Ganymede in 1610. Scientists discovered an ocean under its surface in 2015.

How long was the **longest human burp** ever recorded?

#57

Excuse me!

a. 30 seconds

b. 50 seconds

c. more than 1 minute

121

Just call me belching Betty!

NOW YOU KNOW!
Cows burp a lot. In fact, they burp so much that the methane gas they release into the air contributes to global warming.

ANSWER: C

more than 1 minute

Instant Genius

A decibel (dB) is a unit of measurement used to explain how loud a sound is.

THE LONGEST BURP EVER RECORDED LASTED FOR 1 MINUTE, 13 SECONDS, AND 57 MILLISECONDS. **An Italian man named Michele Forgione set a Guinness World Record for it in a competition in Reggiolo, Italy, in 2009.** Every time you eat or talk quickly, drink through a straw, or even chew gum, you're swallowing little bits of air. **Burping is your body's way of releasing gas that results from swallowing all that air.** The loudest burp ever recorded was 109.9 decibels—about as loud as a running chain saw!

#58

How many **dimples** does a typical **golf ball** have?

a. between 100 and 110

b. between 220 and 300

c. between 300 and 500

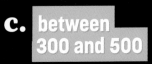

between 300 and 500

SOME OF THE FIRST GOLF BALLS EVER CREATED WERE MADE OF FEATHERS WRAPPED IN LEATHER. **By the 19th century, golf balls were made of dried sap from the sapodilla tree,** which is native to the Caribbean, Mexico, and Central America. **When the rubber core golf ball was invented, in 1899, golf balls started to get uniformly dimpled. The 300 to 500 tiny dimples on the ball's exterior give golfers more control of the ball's movement when they strike it with a club.** It also helps to hit the ball farther. Today, balls used in professional golf must be a specific size and weight, and they must have perfectly symmetrical dimples on their surface.

Instant Genius

Tiger Woods made his first hole in one when he was just eight years old.

Early golf ball

124

Time to go!

#59

How often do
sloths
poop?

a. once an hour   **b.** once a day   **c.** once a week

ANSWER: c   once a week

SLOTHS ARE TREE DWELLERS AND ONE OF THE SLOWEST-MOVING ANIMALS ON EARTH. In general, they lumber about 120 feet (37 m) a day through the trees of the Central and South American forests they call home, where they munch on buds, leaves, and shoots. **It can take a sloth one month to digest a single leaf, so it's no wonder they go to the bathroom only once a week! To do their business, a sloth moves down from its tree and onto the ground.** This takes a lot of energy and makes the animal vulnerable to predators such as jaguars, snakes, and birds of prey such as eagles. Why? Because sloths are even slower on the ground: **There, it takes them about one minute to move just 1 foot (30.5 cm)!**

Instant Genius
Sloths spend up to 90 percent of their time hanging upside down.

Why do stars twinkle?

a. to burn off heat

c. They don't actually twinkle at all.

b. because of light reflected from the moon

Sirius

ANSWER: **C**

They don't actually twinkle at all.

TO OUR EYES, VISIBLE STARS IN THE NIGHT SKY APPEAR TO TWINKLE. But they're not actually blinking on and off; Earth's atmosphere just makes it look like they are. **As the light from a star travels to Earth, the atmosphere bends it, causing the light to bounce and bump around in different directions.** That bouncing, bumping light is what our eyes perceive as twinkling stars.

NOW YOU KNOW!
If you were to look at the stars from a spaceship above Earth's atmosphere, the stars wouldn't twinkle at all.

128

How long did it take
ancient Egyptians
to make a mummy?

a. **70 minutes**

b. **70 hours**

c. **70 days**

That's a wrap.

129

ANCIENT EGYPTIANS BELIEVED THEY HAD TO PRESERVE DEAD BODIES SO THAT PEOPLE WHO HAD PASSED AWAY COULD USE THEM IN THE AFTERLIFE. After a person died, their body would be transformed into a mummy by a special priest. **Mummification was a very long process, taking more than two months from start to finish. First, part of the brain was removed** with a hook inserted through the nose and discarded. **Then, the lungs, intestines, stomach, and liver** were removed and placed inside jars. **The heart was also taken out but later put back into the body and the body was covered in salt for 70 days to preserve it.** Finally, the body was stuffed with linen to give it shape. **It was then wrapped in bandages and stored in a special coffin called a sarcophagus.**

Instant Genius

Ancient Egyptians mummified animals, too.

130

When faced with danger, how does the ant species *Myrmecina graminicola* respond?

62

Row, row, row your boat...

a. It transforms into a wheel.

c. It sings a song.

b. It plays dead.

0.5 mm

It transforms into a wheel.

MYRMECINA GRAMINICOLA **IS THE ONLY ANT SPECIES KNOWN TO TUCK ITSELF INTO A LITTLE BALL AND ROLL AWAY WHEN IT'S IN DANGER.** In fact, this ant is one of the only animals in the world known to use this escape strategy. **When faced with an enemy like a big spider, this tiny insect will bend down its head, balance on its mandible and front antennae, and push off on its hind legs for a jolt of momentum.** This fancy move propels the ant about 80 times faster than if it had walked away.

Instant Genius
Myrmecina graminicola is the size of a sesame seed.

Bagel with sesame seeds

#63

What percentage of people in the world have **brown eyes?**

a. 25 to 30 percent

b. 45 to 50 percent

c. 55 to 80 percent

BROWN IS BY FAR THE MOST COMMON EYE COLOR IN THE WORLD.
The majority of people in Africa, East Asia, and Southeast Asia have dark brown eyes; many people in Europe, the Americas, and Western Asia have light brown eyes. Blue is the next most common eye color, with between 8 and 10 percent of people around the world having blue eyes. Most Scandinavian people (those who live in the northern European countries of Norway, Denmark, Finland, and Sweden) have blue eyes. Only 2 percent of people worldwide have green eyes, making it the least common eye color. Because you inherit physical traits from your parents, it's likely that your eye color will be similar to one or both of theirs.

NOW YOU KNOW!
Animal eye color can vary among species and even within some species. Male box turtles generally have red eyes. Copperhead snakes have yellow eyes.

True or False:

All tigers have the same stripe patterns.

#64

135

Did you say waterslide!

ANSWER: False

TIGERS ARE FAMOUS FOR THEIR ORANGE FUR WITH DARK STRIPES BECAUSE THEY ARE THE ONLY BIG CAT SPECIES WITH THIS DISTINCTIVE COAT. The stripes help tigers camouflage themselves in the tropical forests and grasslands of Asia where they live. As it moves, a tiger's striped coat may resemble moving shadows in the tall grass. Like fingerprints, each tiger has a unique set of markings, which are different on the cat's left and right sides. If you were to shave off a tiger's fur, the big cat would still appear striped! Their hair follicles are so deeply rooted in their skin that they would still clearly display the tiger's unique pattern.

NOW YOU KNOW!

A tiger's tail can be 3 feet (0.9 m) long. It is used for balance and also to communicate. For example, if a tiger is relaxed, its tail hangs loosely.

How many gallons of water do you use during a shower?

a. 10 gallons (38 L)

b. 20 gallons (76 L)

c. 40 gallons (151 L)

#65

ANSWER: **b** **20 gallons (76 L)**

THE TYPICAL SHOWERHEAD SPOUTS OUT AROUND 2.5 GALLONS (9 L) OF WATER A MINUTE. Most people take about eight minutes in the shower. In this amount of time, about 20 gallons (76 L) of water is used, not including the water that's released from the showerhead while waiting for the water temperature to warm up. And **warming water uses a lot of energy!** This is because water needs to absorb a lot of heat before it gets warms up.

NOW YOU KNOW!
You can save 8 gallons (30 L) of water a day by turning off the faucet while you brush your teeth.

What is a **monotreme?**

a. a train with one rail

#66

b. a musical instrument with one hole

c. a mammal without a belly button

139

No lint in my belly button.

ANSWER: C

a mammal without a belly button

THERE ARE THREE TYPES OF MAMMALS. The first is the placental mammal. Humans, dogs, and cats are all examples of this type. Placental mammals develop inside their mothers and are born fully developed. All placental mammals have belly buttons, which form after the umbilical cord, a tubelike object that delivers nutrients from a mother to an unborn baby, is removed. **The second type of mammal is the marsupial.** Kangaroos, koalas, wallabies, and opossums are all marsupials. They're not fully developed at birth, so they move up to their mother's pouch to continue growing. **The third type of mammal is the monotreme.** The platypus and four species of echidnas are the only monotremes. Unlike the other mammals, monotremes lay eggs rather than give birth. Because they do not grow inside their mothers' wombs, monotremes don't need umbilical cords, so they don't have belly buttons.

#67

Ketchup
was once sold
as medicine.

NOW YOU KNOW!
Ketchup is used on pizza in Lebanon and Poland. In Canada, it's used in a frosted dessert called ketchup cake.

ANSWER: True

THE CONDIMENT WE LOVE TO SQUIRT ON BURGERS AND FRIES ORIGINATED MANY CENTURIES AGO IN CHINA AS A FISH-BASED SAUCE CALLED "KE-CHIAP." By the 19th century, the sour, salty sauce had made its way to America. **In 1834, tomatoes, sugar, and spices were added to the recipe, which was sold as a medicine.** The claim was that this special recipe could help with stomach ailments and even some diseases. Of course, claims were not supported by science, and by 1850 ketchup was back where it started: as a sauce. **Today, ketchup is one of the most popular condiments in the world.**

Instant Genius
The most popular condiment in the United States is mayonnaise.

#68

There is
no such
thing as a
**pink
lake.**

143

Lake Hillier, Western Australia

ANSWER: **False**

ON AN ISLAND OFF THE SOUTH COAST OF WESTERN AUSTRALIA THERE'S A LAKE THAT'S ACTUALLY AS PINK AS BUBBLE GUM. The secret to Lake Hillier's color is its saltiness: It is 10 times saltier than the ocean. The combination of heat from sunlight and the high salt content causes the salty water to produce a special type of algae that makes a pinkish pigment. **Because the lake is so salty, no animals live in it—they wouldn't be able to survive.** Amazingly, Lake Hillier is not the only pink lake in the world. Other pink (and even purple) lakes exist throughout Australia, as well as in the countries of Tanzania, Senegal, Russia, Turkey, Spain, and Bolivia.

69

Has anyone seen my toothbrush?

Where was the first

T. rex fossil

found?

a. Argentina

b. the United States

c. Tanzania

the United States

T. REX WAS DISCOVERED IN HELL CREEK, MONTANA, U.S.A. IN 1902, BY PALEONTOLOGIST BARNUM BROWN, WHO WORKED FOR THE AMERICAN MUSEUM OF NATURAL HISTORY IN NEW YORK CITY. **His find took three years to fully excavate, and everyone was shocked at what they had dug up:** a huge dinosaur unlike anything anyone had ever seen before. The bones were packed up and taken to New York by train, where scientists put the pieces of the dinosaur together. It was then that **Tyrannosaurus rex got its name, which means the "tyrant king."** *T. rex* went on display at the American Museum of Natural History in 1906 and was a popular attraction.

Instant Genius
Almost all dinosaurs laid eggs.

American Museum of Natural History, New York City

True or False:

There are more **rats** than people in New York City.

147

FOR A LONG TIME, IT WAS THOUGHT THAT THERE WERE MORE RATS THAN PEOPLE LIVING IN THE BIG APPLE. But that myth was recently busted by a statistician, a person who gathers, analyzes, and interprets data to help us understand new information. **He estimated that the city has around 2 million rats, compared to about 8 million people.** This means that there are four humans for every rat in the city! **New York City is a very hospitable place for rodents because it has lots of garbage, tons of densely packed buildings, and underground tunnels, which are great hiding places for rats.**

Instant Genius

Rats live in colonies of about 40 to 50 members and often travel in packs.

#71

What is the **largest muscle** in your body?

a. your triceps

b. your gluteus maximus

c. your heart

149

your gluteus maximus

YOU'RE SITTING ON IT! YOUR BEHIND, KNOWN TECHNICALLY AS YOUR GLUTEUS MAXIMUS, IS THE LARGEST MUSCLE AND PART OF THE HEAVIEST MUSCLE GROUP IN THE HUMAN BODY. **The buttocks contain three different muscles: the gluteus maximus, the gluteus medius, and the gluteus minimus.** Together, they're known as your glutes. Your glutes evolved to be big and heavy to give you strength and force. **They have many important jobs related to important daily movements,** such as walking and rising from a sitting position, keeping your body in an upright position, enabling you to bolt up the stairs or dash to class, and so much more.

Instant Genius

There are more than 650 muscles in the human body.

Glutes

Why are robins' eggs blue?

#72

a. because of its mother's blood

b. because of its mother's diet

c. because of the material in its nest

NOW YOU KNOW!
Some birds even have speckled, brownish eggs that can blend into the nest, protecting them from predators.

ANSWER: **a**

because of its mother's blood

A ROBIN EGG'S SIGNATURE BLUE COLOR COMES FROM PIGMENTS IN THE MOTHER ROBIN'S BLOOD, WHICH ARE CARRIED TO THE PLACE IN HER BODY WHERE THE EGGSHELL FORMS. Depending on the species, **bird eggs come in a variety of colors, both light and dark,** which allow them to absorb just the right amount of warmth from the sun. **Birds that typically lay eggs in open areas often have lighter-colored eggshells.** Because lighter colors reflect heat from the sun, less of the sun's rays are drawn to them. Eggs laid in shaded, wooded areas are usually darker. Because darker objects absorb more light, these eggs can get the most from the sun's heat that filters through the trees. Many other birds—including blue jays, mynahs, and gray catbirds—also lay blue eggs.

Instant Genius

Adult robins have about 2,900 feathers.

True or False:

A bag of
moon rocks
once sold at auction for $1.8 million.

#73

LUNAR SAMPLE RETURN

Apollo 11 mission

Neil Armstrong's footprint

APOLLO 11

ANSWER: True

AT A 2017 AUCTION CELEBRATING THE 48TH ANNIVERSARY OF THE FIRST MANNED MISSION TO THE MOON, A ZIPPERED BAG OF MOON ROCKS STAMPED WITH THE WORDS "LUNAR SAMPLE RETURN" SOLD FOR $1.8 MILLION. Before the auction, NASA tried to get the rocks back from the woman who was in possession of them by going to court. She herself had previously bought the rocks at an auction for only $995 because the bag that held the rocks was confused with another bag. Unfortunately for NASA, the court did not rule in their favor and the woman was allowed to keep the space souvenirs until she sold them in the 2017 auction. **The rocks were brought to Earth by Neil Armstrong after the Apollo 11 mission to the moon in 1969.**

True or False:

The **Inca people** of South America used potatoes to measure time.

#74

One potato, two potato, three potato...

ANSWER: **True**

POTATOES WERE FIRST GROWN BY THE INCA, INDIANS WHO ONCE RULED ALONG THE WESTERN PART OF SOUTH AMERICA IN THE AREAS THAT ARE NOW PARTS OF ECUADOR, PERU, BOLIVIA, CHILE, AND ARGENTINA. The Inca found many uses for potatoes. **Besides eating them, they used potatoes to mend broken bones and even to tell time. Blocks of time were measured by how long it took to boil a potato.** The Inca also built Machu Picchu, a group of about 200 stone structures located high in the Andes Mountains of modern-day Peru. The building of Machu Picchu is considered an incredible architectural achievement and it is now protected by Peru and the United Nations for its cultural and historical significance.

Instant Genius
The potato was the first vegetable to be grown in space.

75

True or False:

A rattlesnake can't hear its own rattle.

What?

157

ANSWER: False

Instant Genius

Human ears are self-cleaning. They produce earwax that naturally filters out dirt and dust.

SNAKES ARE EARLESS, SO IT WAS LONG ASSUMED THAT THEY COULDN'T HEAR. But scientists discovered that snakes do hear in their own way. In humans, sound waves traveling through the air cause vibrations that reach the eardrum, allowing us to hear. **Although snakes don't have ears or eardrums, they do have ear structures inside their heads.** The structures connect directly to a snake's jawbone, allowing it to pick up vibrations on the ground that send signals to the snake's brain. **As a snake moves along the ground, it can detect the movement of prey and be alerted when predators are nearby.**

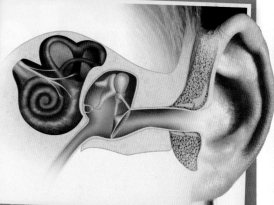

76

True or False:

There are no roads for cars in Venice, Italy.

WATER TAXI

ANSWER: True

THE CITY OF VENICE WAS BUILT ON 118 ISLANDS IN NORTHERN ITALY DURING THE FIFTH CENTURY, AFTER THE FALL OF THE ROMAN EMPIRE. Back then, the area was not much more than a muddy, marshy lagoon with islands in the Adriatic Sea. The earliest settlers dug canals and lined them with wooden stakes. Wooden platforms were constructed on top of the stakes, and buildings were constructed on top of the platforms. As the city was built, materials were moved around on boats in the canals. These canals are still used today and are the main means of transportation around the city. You won't find people getting around Venice by car: Instead, locals and tourists can take gondolas, water taxis, ferries, and boat buses from place to place. Some 400 bridges also cross the many canals lining the city.

How wide is the span of a cat's whiskers?

a. as wide as its body

b. as wide as its tail

c. as wide as every other cat's whiskers

#77

Time to go to the barber.

161

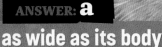

ANSWER: a

as wide as its body

MOST CATS HAVE 12 WHISKERS ON EACH CHEEK THAT ARE ARRANGED IN 4 ROWS OF 3, FOR A TOTAL OF 24 WHISKERS. Cats also have more whiskers around their eyes, ears, jaws, and front legs. **Whiskers are at least as wide as a cat's body, and they are important because, like antennae on insects, whiskers help a cat find its way around.** They are built-in sensory tools, with each whisker rooted three times more deeply in a cat's skin than regular cat hair. **By brushing up against things, whiskers can help cats detect what's around them.** They also make a cat's whiskers very sensitive to changes in its environment, including changes in the air.

NOW YOU KNOW!

Cats can also use their whiskers to communicate. A nervous cat will pin its whiskers back. Relaxed whiskers mean a relaxed cat. A curious kitty will move its whiskers forward.

When was the first video game invented?

a. 1958   b. 1978   c. 1998   #78

Tennis For Two modificato, 1959

COMPUTER TENNIS

PULSE HEIGHT ANALYZER

ELECTRONIC COUNTERS

ANSWER: a 1958

Game controller

THE WORLD'S FIRST VIDEO GAME IS THOUGHT TO HAVE BEEN INVENTED BY A PHYSICIST IN 1958. William Higinbotham was an electronics technician who worked at the Brookhaven National Laboratory in Long Island, New York. **Tasked with creating an exhibition to entertain people on visitors' day, his group created a computer program that could display curves, like the arc of a bouncing ball, for example.** To make his subject more interesting for his demonstration, he made **an interactive game that two people could play called "Tennis for Two."** Players adjusted a knob to control the angle of the ball and pressed a button to hit it toward the other player. It was a huge hit, and the video game was born.

#79

Your bones

are stronger than concrete.

165

HUMAN BONES ARE ABOUT FOUR TIMES STRONGER THAN CONCRETE. The femur in your thigh is the strongest bone in your body because of its long shape and large size. Bones need to be strong because they support the body, as is the case with the femur, and they protect the body's organs. The skull protects the brain, the backbone protects the spinal cord, the ribs shelter the heart and lungs, and the pelvis buffers the bladder and the intestines. **Two main materials make up our bones. Collagen, a protein, is soft and provides a kind of structure for bones. Calcium, a mineral, makes bones hard and strong.**

NOW YOU KNOW!
On each human hand, 14 bones make up the fingers and 8 bones make up each wrist.

True or False:

You can determine the **age of a fish** by counting its scales.

When's my birthday?

#80

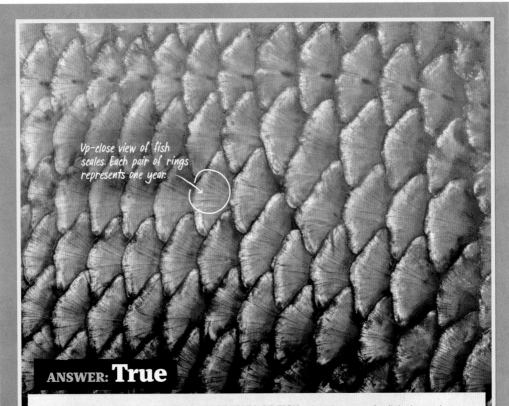

Up-close view of fish scales. Each pair of rings represents one year.

ANSWER: True

THERE ARE ABOUT 32,000 KNOWN SPECIES OF FISH. The life span of a fish depends on the species: **Some deep-sea fish, such as the orange roughy, can live to be 175 years old.** How do scientists know this? **In the same way trees form new growth rings each year, fish develop growth rings on their scales. Each pair of rings represents one year, so scientists can count them to figure out a fish's age. These rings—called annuli—are also found on turtles, earthworms, and leeches.** In the summer, the rings on fish scales are farther apart because fish grow faster in warmer weather. During winter, the rings are closer together, because in the cold, fish eat less and grow more slowly.

What's the **dirtiest item** in your kitchen?

#81

a. the floor

b. the sponge

c. the dog's bowl

169

Bacteria are a grayish blue color, and other microorganisms are green in this extreme close-up of a kitchen sponge.

ANSWER: b
the sponge

A KITCHEN SPONGE HAS MORE BACTERIA THAN A TOILET SEAT. In fact, dishcloths and sponges are dirtier than any other item in the average home! **A recent study found that 362 different kinds of bacteria live in the crevices of sponges.** How does this happen? Well, bacteria grow in sponges when they don't fully dry. **A typical kitchen sponge can have trillions of microscopic bacteria on it.** So, it's important to wash your sponge after each use and put it somewhere it can dry completely. **You can also wash sponges in a dishwasher to help get rid of anything gross.**

Instant Genius
Bacteria live all over the world.

There are no
volcanoes
under the ocean.

#82

West Mata volcano

Remote undersea vehicle

ANSWER: **False**

MORE THAN 70 PERCENT OF EARTH'S VOLCANIC ACTIVITY HAPPENS DEEP IN THE OCEAN. Submarine volcanoes erupt from cracks in the ocean floor. Scientists who study volcanoes find these eruptions very helpful because, aboveground, it's not possible to get close to a volcano, especially when it's erupting. **Under the sea, however, the water pressure helps hold back the force of an explosion. Thanks to technology and remotely operated vehicles (ROVs), scientists can get closer to an erupting submarine volcano to study the explosion of lava, gases, ash, and rock.** Experts think there are more than one million underwater volcanoes, although most are extinct—meaning they haven't erupted in at least tens of thousands of years and are not expected to erupt again.

At any given time, how many **insects** are alive?

a. millions

b. billions

c. quintillions

ANSWER: C **quintillions**

SCIENTISTS ESTIMATE THAT THERE ARE ABOUT 10 QUINTILLION (10,000,000,000,000,000,000) INSECTS CRAWLING AROUND OUR PLANET.

Scientists have named around 900,000 different species of insects, but they think there could be anywhere from 2 to 30 million species in existence. Why are there so many bugs on Earth? There are lots of reasons, including the fact that many are small and some have the ability to fly, which helps them survive different types of environments and allows them to more easily escape danger. **One major factor is that insects have babies at whopping rates. For example, a female East African termite can lay 43,000 eggs in a single day!**

Instant Genius

Insects breathe through holes on the sides of their bodies called spiracles.

Help!

A swarm of locusts

How many
layers are in
Earth's
atmosphere?

a. 5   b. 7   c. 10

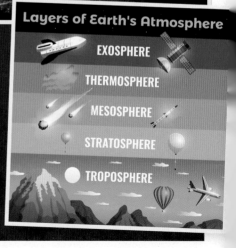

ANSWER: a   **5**

EARTH'S ATMOSPHERE IS MADE UP OF FIVE LAYERS. Starting at the surface, the first layer is the troposphere. This is where we live and where all weather occurs. **Above the troposphere is the stratosphere.** This is where weather balloons known as radiosondes float and where the ozone layer is. **The mesosphere is the third and coldest layer of Earth's atmosphere.** Meteors burn up in this layer. **Higher up is the thermosphere, where the aurora borealis (northern lights) and the aurora australis (southern lights) happen and where the Kármán line is found.** (The Kármán line is an imaginary boundary that marks the start of space, about 62 miles (100 km) above Earth's surface.) **The fifth and final layer is the exosphere, where some satellites orbit our planet.**

Layers of Earth's Atmosphere

EXOSPHERE

THERMOSPHERE

MESOSPHERE

STRATOSPHERE

TROPOSPHERE

True or False:

#85

Shivering

is a way your body produces heat when you're cold.

ANSWER: True

IF YOUR BODY IS COLD, IT REACTS BY SHIVERING AND BY SLOWING THE BLOOD FLOW TO YOUR HANDS AND FEET, ALSO KNOWN AS YOUR EXTREMITIES. When your body shivers, your muscles are shaking as a way to produce heat. When your body slows the blood flow to your extremities, **the blood that would have reached them is sent to your most important organs instead.** This ensures that those vital organs—such as the brain, heart, and lungs—stay warm.

Oh...no! My nose.

NOW YOU KNOW!

Your nose gets warmer when you lie. Scientists call it the Pinocchio effect after the fictional character whose nose grew when he told a lie.

#86

True or False:

Fortune cookies

Don't eat the paper.

have contained winning lottery numbers.

179

better soon.

ove is being stupid together.

ANSWER: **True**

IN 2019, A NORTH CAROLINA MAN WON MORE THAN $340 MILLION IN A LOTTERY AFTER USING NUMBERS THAT WERE LISTED ON A FORTUNE COOKIE HIS GRANDDAUGHTER BROUGHT OVER AFTER EATING AT A LOCAL RESTAURANT. And it wasn't even the first time a fortune cookie had offered this kind of luck: **in 2015, a Florida man won a $10 million lottery jackpot the same way!** Fortune cookies are served in many Chinese restaurants in the United States, though the treat is thought to have originated in Japan.

NOW YOU KNOW!

Before fortune cookies are baked, the dough is flattened into circles. When they're cooked, fortunes are placed on each cookie and the cookies are folded over while they're still hot. Then they cool and harden with the fortunes inside.

How long do
koalas
sleep each day?

87

That was a big dinner!

a. **up to 10 hours**

b. **up to 18 hours**

c. **up to 20 hours**

ANSWER: b

up to 18 hours

KOALAS LIVE IN THE EUCALYPTUS FORESTS OF EASTERN AUSTRALIA, WHERE THE LEAVES OF EUCALYPTUS TREES ARE THEIR MAIN SOURCE OF FOOD. They can eat more than 2 pounds (1 kg) of leaves a day! Eucalyptus leaves are poisonous for most other animals, but koalas produce special chemicals that remove the poisons. However, because these leaves don't provide much nutrition, a koala's digestive system works overtime to take in nutrients and get rid of the toxins found in these leaves. **For this reason—and because a good chunk of their energy goes to digesting this hard-to-digest food—koalas spend up to 18 hours a day sleeping.**

China won more gold medals than any other country during the 2008 summer Olympics in Beijing.

#88

ANSWER: **True**

IN 2008, CHINA HOSTED THE SUMMER OLYMPIC GAMES IN BEIJING. Chinese athletes had competed in numerous Olympic Games, but 2008 was the first time China had athletes competing in all 28 sports. **That year, the country won a total of 100 medals, including 48 gold, 22 silver, and 30 bronze.** Multiple gold medals were awarded in shooting, diving, weightlifting, gymnastics, judo, badminton, and table tennis. China came in first for the most gold medals won during the Beijing Olympic Games and second after the United States for most metals won overall during the 2008 games.

True or False:

Adults and babies have the same number of bones.

#89

ANSWER: **False**

ADULTS HAVE 206 BONES. BUT AS BABIES, HUMANS ARE ALL BORN WITH ABOUT 300. As newborns grow, smaller bones eventually fuse together to make bigger, stronger ones. **Bones continue to grow until a person is about 20 years old.** A child's bones are more flexible and can heal quicker than adult bones because they have a different chemical makeup. **Children's bones might bend or "bow" instead of breaking. As we become adults and our bones are fully developed, instead of flexing they are more likely to snap and break with force.** The arm and collarbone are the most commonly broken bones.

Hawaii

is moving about 4 inches (10 cm) closer to Japan every year.

#90

ANSWER: True

HAWAII IS ABOUT 4,000 MILES (6,400 KM) FROM THE JAPANESE ISLAND OF HOKKAIDO. But it's inching closer every year. **This is because Hawaii and Japan are on different tectonic plates.** Tectonic plates are like giant puzzle pieces of land that connect Earth's outer shell. **The seven major plates that form Earth's crust are constantly moving: At the current rate of movement, Hawaii could reach Japan in 63 million years.** But scientists aren't so sure that will actually happen. Although Earth's plates have moved in the same direction for millions of years at a time, they could still change direction in the very distant future.

Instant Genius
Hawaii is made up of 8 main islands and 124 small islands, called islets.

91

Who turned out the lights?

What happens inside a **butterfly chrysalis?**

a. The caterpillar digests itself.

b. The caterpillar attracts a butterfly.

c. The caterpillar deposits an egg.

ANSWER: a

The caterpillar digests itself.

AFTER A CATERPILLAR HATCHES FROM AN EGG, IT IS VERY HUNGRY. **For anywhere between 5 and 21 days, it eats and eats and eats leaves.** Then, one day, the caterpillar stops and finds a safe branch where it can hang upside down. **There, it spins a protective chrysalis as a temporary home in which it will transform into a butterfly. Inside the chrysalis, the caterpillar releases special chemicals to turn itself into a soupy substance.** Cells in this protein-rich liquid will grow into the butterfly's wings, eyes, antennae, and other body parts. The transformation is complete within 9 to 14 days, at which point the butterfly emerges from the chrysalis, waits for its wings to dry, and flies away.

Instant Genius

Butterflies get vitamins by drinking from mud puddles.

Which of these **animals has a diet** that is most like a human's?

a. cat

b. bird

c. pig

BELIEVE IT OR NOT, PIGS AND HUMANS HAVE MANY PHYSICAL SIMILARITIES. Pigs can develop the same diseases as humans, and they also have the same type of immune systems to fight off sickness. **Like humans, pigs have one stomach.** (Some animals, including cows and sheep, have a stomach with four compartments.) **The placement of a number of pig organs is also similar to the placement of organs in the human body.** Pigskin and human skin are also similar in structure. And like humans, pigs are omnivores: **They can eat anything because their bodies can convert both meat and plants into nutrients.** Because our bodies are so similar, doctors have even used skin and heart valves from pigs to heal humans.

Instant Genius

Wild pigs can run really fast—about 30 miles (48 km) an hour!

Better than air conditioning!

NOW YOU KNOW!

Pigs cover themselves with mud to keep cool because they don't have sweat glands, just like rhinos!

What is the origin of saying "God bless you" after someone sneezes?

a. to pray away evil spirits

b. to show manners

c. to trap germs

NOW
YOU KNOW!
Sneezing is a powerful
human action, blasting
mucus and air from the
nose and mouth at up to
10 miles (16 km)
an hour.

ANSWER: a

to pray away evil spirits

A SNEEZE IS YOUR BODY'S RESPONSE TO SOMETHING IRRITATING THE INSIDE OF YOUR NOSE.
**Your nerve endings send a signal to your brain, which tells your body to take a deep breath and hold
it. This builds up pressure in your lungs, which then shoots your breath and whatever was irritating
your nose out of your body.** Historically, before we understood sneezing, there was superstition
around it. Some people believed that sneezing made your heart stop. **Others thought sneezes cast
out evil spirits from the body.** This belief about spirits existed in cultures all over the world. Today
we know that a sneeze can contain germs that can get you and others sick with the cold or flu.
Sneezes can also contain materials that cause allergies, such as dust. **If you feel a sneeze coming
on, always catch it in your elbow and not your hands, which can spread germs easier.**

Which of these animals has the
longest life span?

c. koi fish

a. tortoise

b. Greenland shark

ANSWER: **b** Greenland shark

ALL OF THESE ANIMALS LIVE EXTREMELY LONG LIVES COMPARED WITH OTHER SPECIES. Koi have an average life span of 40 years. A tortoise's average life span is about 175 years. And the winner for the most birthday candles is the Greenland shark, which can live some 400 years! How do scientists know the age of Greenland sharks? They discovered a protein in the eyes of these sharks that forms at birth and doesn't age. Scientists were able to date these proteins to figure out how old the sharks are.

NOW YOU KNOW!

The Greenland shark is one of the larger shark species. It can grow up to 20 feet (6 m) long and weigh about 2,200 pounds (1,000 kg).

Which is colder:

the North Pole or the South Pole?

a. the North Pole

b. the South Pole

c. It's a tie.

ANSWER: **b**

the South Pole

THE SOUTH POLE HAS AVERAGE TEMPERATURES OF MINUS 18° F (–28° C) IN THE SUMMER AND MINUS 76° F (–60° C) IN THE WINTER. The North Pole doesn't get as cold, with average temperatures reaching 32° F (0° C) in the summer and minus 40° F (–40° C) in the winter. **Though both poles are *frrreeezing,* the South Pole is colder because it sits on top of a very thick ice sheet and has mountains.** Because mountains have a higher elevation, they stay very cold, and temperatures on a mountaintop are usually even colder than the land below. **Something both poles have in common is that sometimes they don't get any direct sunlight—another reason for the frigid temperatures.**

#96

A sea star
can grow back a limb.

Pacific Ocean, British Columbia, Canada

ANSWER: **True**

SEA STARS ARE INVERTEBRATES—ANIMALS THAT DON'T HAVE BACKBONES. More than 1,900 species of sea stars live on ocean floors all over the world. Some are about the size of your pinkie nail; others are much bigger. **The sunflower sea star, one of the largest, has an arm span of more than 3 feet (1 m)!** Sea stars have the ability to regrow their arms. Most sea star species need at least part of their main body to be intact to do this, which can take a year or more. **Amazingly, some species can regrow an entirely new body from just a single limb!**

NOW YOU KNOW!
A sea star's arm has about 15,000 tiny "feet" that enable it to walk across the ocean floor.

200

#97

China is spending $3 million to build panda-shaped solar farms.

First solar power station shaped like a panda, Datong City, China

ANSWER: **False**

CHINA IS ACTUALLY SPENDING $3 BILLION TO BUILD THESE SOLAR FARMS. The idea came from a 15-year-old student in Hong Kong who wanted to get people interested in renewable energy to help the environment. The first panda-shaped solar farm was built in 2017, and created enough energy to power about 10,000 homes a year. China's goal is to build 100 panda solar farms across the country.

#98

True or False:

Bats
pollinate flowers.

Time for my afternoon siesta!

Bats can fly at speeds of up to
60 miles (97 km) an hour.

ANSWER: **True**

IN DESERT AND TROPICAL AREAS,
BATS HELP THE ENVIRONMENT BY
POLLINATING FLOWERS, WHICH
HELP NEW FLOWERS GROW. When a
bat drinks nectar from a flower, pollen
sticks to the hairs on its body. Then the
pollen falls on the next flower it drinks
from. This process continues as bats
fly from one flower to the next. **While
at a flower, bats will not only drink the
nectar but also eat any insects that
might be there, too.** They'll also eat
parts of the flower itself.

NOW
YOU KNOW!
Sometimes bat poop
sparkles because of a
shiny substance found
in the insects
they eat.

#99

What causes your foot to "fall asleep"?

a. You've cut off blood circulation to it.

b. You've pressed on a nerve, so your brain can't communicate with it.

c. Too much blood is flowing to it.

205

> **Instant Genius**
>
> The human body has billions of nerve cells.

> **NOW YOU KNOW!**
>
> The human spinal cord transmits nerve signals at 268 miles (431 km) an hour.

ANSWER: b

You've pressed on a nerve, so your brain can't communicate with it.

AFTER YOU'VE BEEN SITTING IN ONE POSITION FOR A LONG TIME, YOU MIGHT FEEL A TINGLING, PINS-AND-NEEDLES SENSATION IN YOUR FOOT. It's just a common case of paresthesia. **Paresthesia happens when a nerve becomes squished and can't properly communicate with the brain.** Without the connection between your brain and foot, you don't feel anything. But this is only temporary. **By simply changing positions, the pressure on your nerve will release and your foot will slowly start to feel normal again.** Moving your foot in a circular motion can speed up the process. **Crossing your legs or falling asleep on your hand or arm can also lead to paresthesia.**

Why can you sometimes see the moon during the day?

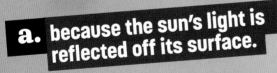

a. because the sun's light is reflected off its surface.

b. because it's bigger than the sun.

c. because it never moves.

207

ANSWER: a

because the sun's light is reflected off its surface.

THE MOON AND THE STARS ARE ALWAYS IN THE SKY, EVEN WHEN WE CAN'T SEE THEM DURING THE DAY. When we can't see the moon, it's between the sun and Earth, and the part of the moon that is lit by the sun is facing away from Earth. When we can see the moon, whether it's day or night, the sun's light is reflecting on it. As the moon orbits around Earth, we see its eight different phases over the period of about a month.

Instant Genius

The moon has an oval-shaped orbit.

Octopuses

can change their appearance in a matter of seconds.

ANSWER: **True**

OCTOPUSES CAN CHANGE THE WAY THEY LOOK TO CAMOUFLAGE THEMSELVES AND HIDE FROM PREDATORS SUCH AS SHARKS.

Octopuses change their color in seconds and can even give themselves patterns to match a particular object or to look like another animal. These highly intelligent creatures also build dens. They will pull in a stone to use as a door and place it at the opening once their soft bodies are safely tucked inside the den.

Cuttlefish

Instant Genius

Squid and cuttlefishes can also quickly change the color of their skin.

Spot the 7 Random Differences:

Turn to page 215 for the answers! **211**

Index

Page numbers in *italic* refer to images.

Photo Credits

Credits

Text and cover design copyright © 2022 by
Penguin Random House LLC

All rights reserved. Published in the United States by Bright Matter
Books, an imprint of Random House Children's Books, a division of
Penguin Random House LLC, New York.

Bright Matter Books and the colophon are registered trademarks of
Penguin Random House LLC.

Visit us on the Web! **rhcbooks.com**

Educators and librarians, for a variety of teaching tools, visit us
at **RHTeachersLibrarians.com**

Library of Congress Cataloging-in-Publication Data is available
upon request.
ISBN 978-0-593-45049-9 (trade)
ISBN 978-0-593-45051-2 (lib. bdg.)
ISBN 978-0-593-51613-3 (ebook)

COVER PHOTO CREDITS:
Front Cover Photo: Shutterstock.
Back Cover Photo: Dreamstime.

MANUFACTURED IN ITALY
10 9 8 7 6 5 4 3 2 1
First Edition

Produced by Fun Factory Press, LLC, in association with
Potomac Global Media, LLC.

The publisher would like to thank the following people for their
contributions to this book: Melina Gerosa Bellows, President,
Fun Factory Press, and Series Creator and Author; Priyanka
Lamichhane, Editor and Project Manager; Chad Tomlinson, Art
Director; Jen Agresta, Copy Editor; Michelle Harris, Fact-checker;
Potomac Global Media: Kevin Mulroy, Publisher; Barbara Brownell
Grogan, Editor in Chief, Christopher L. Mazzatenta, Designer;
Susannah Jayes and Ellen Dupont, Picture Researchers; Jane
Sunderland and Heather McElwain, Contributing Editors